Chapter 5

Interactions in Ecosystems

You Will Discover

- what an ecosystem is.
- what land biomes are like.
- what water ecosystems are like.
- how organisms interact in an ecosystem.
- how energy moves through an ecosystem.
- how materials move through an ecosystem.

online Student Edition
pearsonsuccessnet.com

Build Background

How do the parts of an ecosystem interact?

ecosystem
community
niche
cycle

habitat

population

Chapter 5 Vocabulary

ecosystem page 127

population page 127

community page 127

niche page 129

habitat page 129

energy pyramid page 146

cycle page 149

energy pyramid

Heat
Heat
Heat
Energy

Lab zone Directed Inquiry

Explore How can you find out how many animals live in an area?

Scientists can figure out how many animals live in a large area by counting how many animals there are in small parts of the area and then estimating. The more small parts they check, the better their estimate usually is.

Materials

checkerboard

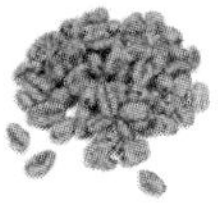

dry puffed cereal

calculator or computer (optional)

What to Do

1. Scatter 2 handfuls of cereal on a checkerboard. Guess how many pieces of cereal there are.
2. Count the number of pieces on 4 squares. Divide by 4. Multiply your answer by the total number of squares. The result is an **estimate** of the total number of pieces.

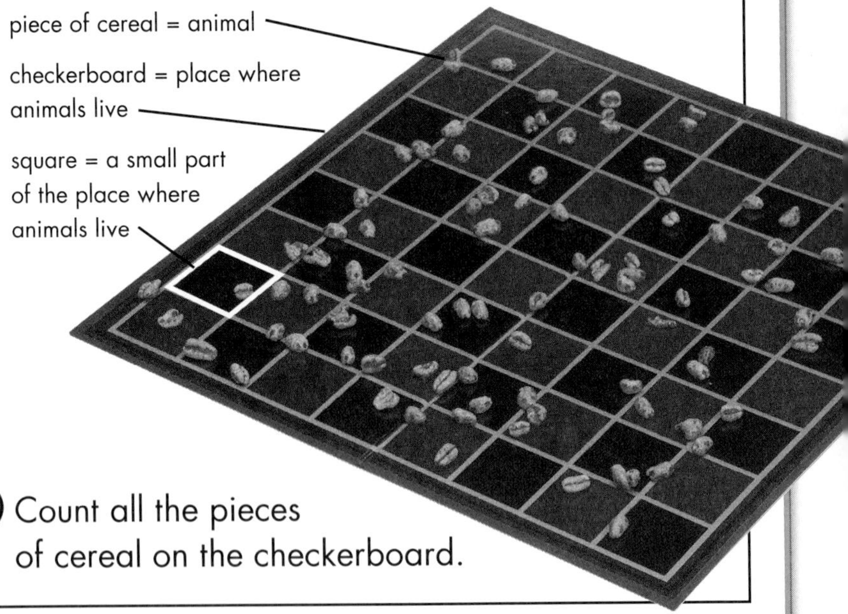

piece of cereal = animal
checkerboard = place where animals live
square = a small part of the place where animals live

3. Count all the pieces of cereal on the checkerboard.

Process Skills

Sometimes you can use mathematics to help you make a good **estimate.**

Explain Your Results

1. Which was easiest: guessing, estimating, or counting? Which was most accurate?
2. How do you think you could make your **estimate** more accurate?

How to Read Science

Reading Skills

Predict

When you **predict,** you make a statement about what you think might happen next. The statement you make is a **prediction.** An **estimate** is a kind of prediction.

- You can make predictions based on what you already know and what has already happened.
- After you predict something in a story or an article, continue reading to check your prediction. As you learn new information, you might need to change your prediction.

Science Article

Habitats

All plants and animals live in a habitat. The ocean is a habitat not only for fish, but for many types of plants, animals, and other organisms. Forests are habitats for foxes, squirrels, birds, and other animals. Sometimes habitats become polluted or destroyed, causing a serious effect on the plants and animals living there.

Apply It!

Make a graphic organizer like the one shown. Make a **prediction** to answer the question from the article.

Question		Prediction
If habitats are polluted or destroyed, what effect might this have on the animals living there?	→	

You Are There!

During a long hike, you stop at a fallen tree to rest. You soon realize that what seemed like a calm, peaceful spot is actually very busy! Squirrels are chasing each other up and down trees. Birds are frightened by the squirrels and fly to another area. At your feet you see a long line of ants carrying food. How does this forest meet the needs of all these animals?

Lesson 1

What is an ecosystem?

Organisms live where they can have their needs met. These needs are met by the living and nonliving things around them.

Where Organisms Live

What kind of ecosystem are you in right now? An **ecosystem** is all the living and nonliving things in an area. An ecosystem is any place that living things are found. Your classroom is an ecosystem.What are the living and nonliving things in your classroom?

Living and Nonliving Parts

Many populations make up the living parts of an ecosystem. A **population** is a group of organisms of one species that live in an area at the same time. A population may be all the oak trees or all the red ants in an area. A **community** is made up of all the populations in an area. Members of a community depend on each other to fill needs, such as food, shelter, and reproduction.

The nonliving parts of an ecosystem include air, water, soil, temperature, and sunlight. They often determine what kinds of organisms and the number of organisms that can live there.

As in any system, the living and nonliving parts of an ecosystem interact in many ways. Each part has a role. In this way, the whole system works to meet the needs of all its parts.

In any ecosystem, some organisms survive; others do not. Populations can live and grow only where their needs are met. If a population's needs are not met, the population will get smaller. Some of its members might move away. Maybe none will survive.

1. **✓Checkpoint** Describe the parts of an ecosystem that organisms need.
2. **Predict** What would happen to a community if half the water from an ecosystem were removed?

Biomes

Biologists have divided the world into regions called biomes. A biome is a large ecosystem with generally the same climate and organisms. A single biome may cover many countries. Together, all the biomes make up the biosphere.

When you hear the word "rainforest," do you think of a hot jungle on the other side of the world? A rainforest biome is any place that has large amounts of rain and thick plant growth. Did you know that there is a rainforest in the state of Washington? It is a temperate rainforest, which means that it receives a lot of rain during the year, but its temperature can be quite cool.

Temperate Rainforest

A temperate rainforest community has trees such as maple and spruce. These grow well in the wet, cool climate. Mosses often cover rocks. Elk, cougars, and bears are some of the animals in the area. Squirrels, raccoons, and owls also live in the temperate rainforest.

Look at the roles of the trees and squirrels in this ecosystem. Trees help squirrels by giving them food and shelter. Squirrels help trees by spreading seeds. These organisms help each other meet their needs.

The squirrels and trees are just two parts of this ecosystem. The whole system works because its parts and organisms interact to meet each others' needs.

Raccoons can use their paws skillfully for climbing and hunting.

Elk use their antlers to defend themselves.

Map Fact

Temperate rainforests are found on the west coast of North America, from Oregon to Alaska. They are also found in other places of the world.

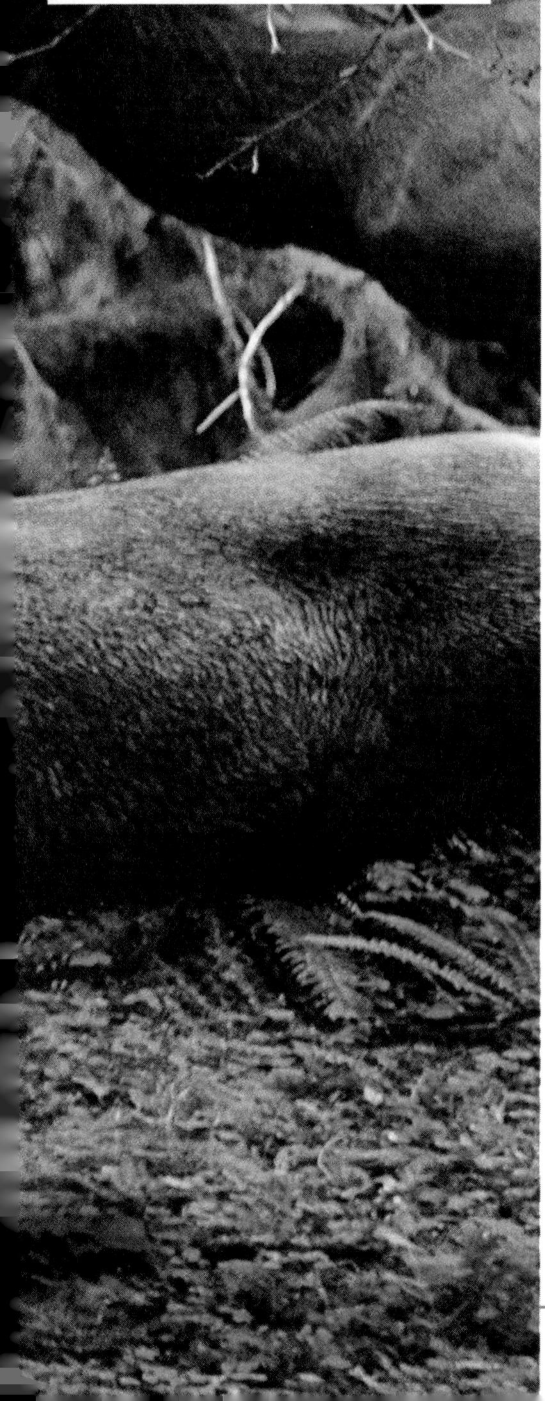

Spotted owls are hunters in temperate rainforests.

Balance in Ecosystems

Every organism in an ecosystem has a niche and a habitat. A **niche** is the role that an organism has in an ecosystem. The niche of a spotted owl in the temperate rainforest is that of a hunter. It eats small animals, such as mice and chipmunks. A **habitat** is the place in which an organism lives. A habitat is made up of the soil, air and water, as well as the plants of the area. The habitats of spotted owls are the trees and the land on which they live.

All the relationships among organisms keep the ecosystem balanced. For instance, the population of spotted owls balances with the populations of small animals, such as mice, that are their food. If the number of small animals drops too low, the owls will have less food. So, their number will decrease too. With fewer owls hunting, fewer mice will be eaten. As a result, the population of mice will grow. Then, when more mice are around, the number of owls will increase again. In this way, the populations of owls and small animals go up and down within a range and they balance.

✓ Lesson Checkpoint

1. What is a population? What determines the kind and size of populations in an area?
2. Describe the parts of an ecosystem and tell how they maintain the system's balance.
3. **Art in Science** Draw a picture of a habitat and label its parts.

Lesson 2

What are land biomes?

Organisms have structures or behaviors that help them live in the different land biomes.

Tropical Rainforest Biomes

Ecosystems near the equator are warm all year long. Some of these places get large amounts of rain. In some parts of Brazil, the average temperature is 26°C, and the average rainfall is more than 3 meters per year. In places like this, many plants can easily have their needs met. As a result, populations of these plants grow very large. A tropical rainforest results.

Tropical rainforests have more species than all other biomes. Dozens of different kinds of flowers and insects may be found on one tree.

Do you think that a rainforest would be the ideal place for any organism to live? In any environment, some organisms survive well, and some do not. Certain plants, such as orchids, survive well. Most kinds of cactus plants would not survive in the wet tropical rainforests.

Organisms have structures that help them survive in their ecosystems. For example, the kinkajou has a tail that can grab onto branches to help it move through the trees. Its long tongue can gather honey and insects to eat.

Map Fact

Tropical rainforests are found on all continents except Europe. The rainforest shown here is in Costa Rica, a country on the continent of North America.

Basilisk lizard

Kinkajou

Map Fact

Deciduous forests are the main biomes found in Europe and the eastern half of the United States of America.

Deciduous Forest Biomes

A deciduous forest may grow in cooler places that do not have huge amounts of rain. Deciduous forests cover large areas of the eastern part of the United States. These forests have trees such as oaks, elms, and maples. Deciduous trees lose their leaves in the colder fall and winter months. Losing leaves helps trees save food and water during the winter.

Besides trees, what organisms undergo some sort of change during cold months? With less food available, bears in the deciduous forest sleep through much of the winter. Snakes, frogs, and salamanders hibernate underground. The fur color of some rabbits changes to a snowy white. If it sees an enemy, the rabbit keeps itself very still and it blends in with the snow.

With the right conditions, such as plenty of food, few diseases, and few predators, a population will continue to increase. This has been seen in populations of deer in deciduous forests. The population of deer has increased so much that in some places, overcrowding is a problem. When overcrowding occurs, food supplies can run out. Then many deer may die of starvation.

1. ✓ **Checkpoint** Give examples of how an organism's behavior is related to changes in the deciduous forest biome.
2. **Math in Science** In a tree in a tropical rainforest, three dozen different flowers and forty-eight different insects were found. How many different species were found in all?

Populations of a deer's natural enemies, such as wolves, have decreased in recent years. This has led to large deer populations.

Grassland Biomes

Two hundred years ago, tall grasses covered huge areas of Midwest America. Some grasses grew to be over two meters tall. Pioneers called this area a sea of grass. Now, most of these grasslands have been turned into farms.

Grasslands are biomes that are covered with many types of grasses and have few trees. Decaying dead grasses form fertile soil. Trees do not grow well in this biome because of the small amount of rain it receives. Most trees in grasslands are near lakes or rivers. Animals such as bison, antelope, and prairie dogs eat the grass. They are hunted by wolves and coyotes.

Populations of animals often decrease when their habitat changes. The change can be in the climate, the number of enemies, or in their food or water supply.

The gray wolf is one species with a changing population. Gray wolves once lived over most of North America. When grasslands were changed into farms, animals such as prairie dogs decreased in number. Wolves then had less food and less space. At the same time, people were hunting wolves more. As a result, gray wolves now live only in lightly populated northern states.

In 1974, gray wolves in the U.S. were found in only three states. People worked for many years to increase their habitat. Most wolves in this species are gray, but some are black or brown.

Map Fact

One large grassland biome extends from Mexico to Canada.

Map Fact

All taigas are in the Northern Hemisphere. This photograph shows a taiga at Denali National Park, Alaska.

Taiga Biomes

Another kind of forest biome covers much of Canada and Russia in places that are cold and fairly dry. In these places, called taigas, most trees are the kind that have needles, such as pines.

Needles have many qualities that help trees survive the cold conditions of the taiga. Needles are leaves that make food for the tree. The tree has needles throughout the year. This way, the tree is ready to make food as soon as it is warm enough for photosynthesis to happen. The needles have a waxy coating. This helps the tree hold water during the winter months.

Some of the animals that are found in taiga communities are bears, elk, moose, and wolves. Some smaller animals in the taiga are mice, porcupines, and wolverines. These animals have fur that helps keep them warm in the cold winters. Ducks, owls, and woodpeckers may be seen in the taigas. Their feathers help keep them warm.

1. **√ Checkpoint** What changes in a habitat would cause a population to decrease?
2. **Technology** in Science Use Internet resources to investigate the taiga and grassland biomes. Compare and contrast the kinds of animals found in the two biomes and their needs.

People in a taiga will sometimes see a moose wading in a stream, gently dipping its head into the water to get a mouthful of plants.

Desert Biomes

What do you think makes a place a desert? Do all deserts have high temperatures and sand dunes? Although many deserts are very hot, they can be much cooler at night. Some can be quite cold most of the time. Not all deserts have sand dunes. Some are very rocky. A desert can also be covered by a very flat layer of salt. So what exactly is a desert? Deserts are often defined as areas that receive less than 25 centimeters of rain or snow each year.

Map Fact

Every continent has deserts. The desert shown here is in western Australia.

Desert Organisms

Desert organisms have special structures and behaviors that help them survive in the dry conditions of many deserts. Some desert plants have large root systems close to the surface of the ground. These roots quickly take up any water from rain. To deal with high temperatures, many animals rest during the day. Some dig into the ground to get cool. They look for food in the cooler temperatures at night.

What desert organisms can you name? Communities of the desert may include rattlesnakes, lizards, jackrabbits, and beetles. Bushes, grasses, and cactuses may grow in deserts as well.

The largest deserts are found in northern Africa and southwest Asia. A large part of western Australia is a desert. What other places are deserts?

Emus are found in many areas of Australia, including deserts. They may travel many kilometers each day to find food and water.

Map Fact

Most tundras are found along the northern coasts of Canada and Russia. Canadian tundra is shown in the picture below.

When snows cover the tundra, caribou often change their grazing behavior and move to warmer areas for food.

Tundra Biomes

The tundra is a very cold biome with little rain. Tundras are generally in the most northern areas of the world. Rodents, rabbits, and caribou feed on small plants and grasses. Weasels, owls, and foxes also live on the tundra.

Carrying Capacity

Certain factors limit the number of organisms that can live in any ecosystem. Limiting factors include the amount of food, water, space, or shelter. A population may grow only to a certain size and still have all its needs met. The number of organisms that can live in a place is called the carrying capacity.

Overcrowding results if a population grows larger than the carrying capacity. Organisms will not be able to meet their needs. They must move to another area or they will not survive.

In the tundra, a major limiting factor is the short time of warm weather. The soil is frozen during all but a few weeks each year. Even then, only the top layer of soil thaws. Plants cannot grow deep roots or tall stems. Trees cannot grow in these conditions. The small plants that grow in the tundra provide less food and shelter for animals than larger plants that grow in warmer forests. What biome has a carrying capacity like the tundra?

√ Lesson Checkpoint

1. Explain how characteristics of an organism help it survive in a desert.
2. What is the effect of a limiting factor on a population?
3. Writing in Science **Persuasive** What biome do you think is the best place to live? In your **science journal,** write an essay to persuade your classmates that your choice is the best.

Lesson 3

What are water ecosystems?

Water ecosystems differ in the kind of water they have, how fast it moves, and how deep it is.

Rivers

What animals are found in a river ecosystem community? You may think of fish right away. Pike, bullhead, and bass are kinds of fish in rivers. Other animals, such as crayfish, otters, ducks, turtles, and insects, are also parts of many river ecosystems.

Different kinds of rivers have different kinds of organisms. Some animals live only in rivers that flow slowly. They are not strong enough to live in rivers that flow very fast. Few organisms of any kind can live in badly polluted waters.

Plants and animals that live in rivers usually do not also live in oceans. Their cells cannot handle the extra salt in ocean water. In the same way, plants and animals that live in the ocean usually cannot live in rivers and lakes.

Water ecosystems include animals that spend much of their time on land. Animals that live on land and in water need structures that allow them to do well in both environments. For example, the streamlined body of the river otter helps it to swim easily and catch fish. While it swims it can close its nose and ears. On land it can run and catch small mammals and frogs. Otters live in holes that they dig at the river's edge.

Map Fact
The Mississippi River, shown here, is the largest river ecosystem in North America. The Amazon, Nile, and Yangtze Rivers are major rivers on other continents.

River otter

Map Fact

The Congaree Swamp is in South Carolina. Many kinds of wetlands are found all over the world.

Wetlands

A wetland is partly covered with water or is flooded at least part of each year. This means that many of the plants and animals of wetlands are found on land and in water.

There are many kinds of wetlands. The wetland of Florida's Everglades has vast areas of sawgrass over 3 meters tall. Alligators, fish, deer, snakes and other animals live there. A swamp is another kind of wetland with many trees and bushes. The Congaree Swamp community in South Carolina has deer, otters, turtles, snakes, and wild pigs.

Wetlands are helpful in many ways. The plants, soils, and microorganisms of wetlands often act as filters, cleaning water that flows through a wetland. This helps all organisms in the water.

Some important wetlands are parts of estuaries. Estuaries are places where rivers flow into oceans. An estuary's water is salty, but not as salty as the ocean. Salt marshes are grassy wetlands at the edges of estuaries. Salt marshes protect inland areas from stormy ocean waves. As the tides change, ocean water flows in and out of a salt marsh. This may change the water levels and the salinity of a salt marsh.

1. **√ Checkpoint** Where are estuaries found?
2. **Technology in Science** Use Internet resources to investigate a river or wetland ecosystem. Write a paragraph that describes how organisms on land and in the water interact with each other and with the habitat.

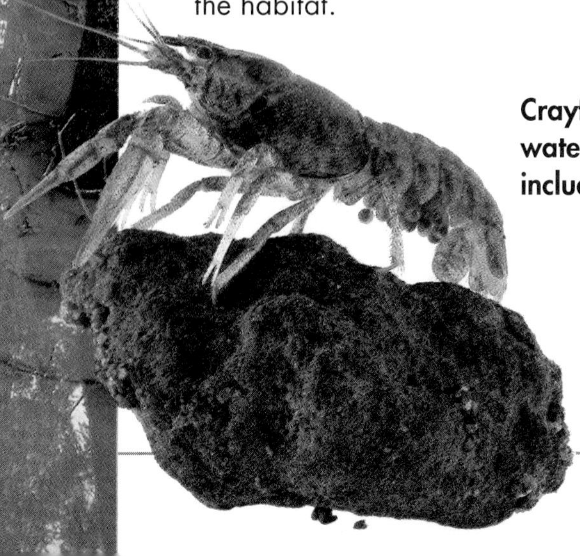

Crayfish live in several water ecosystems, including swamps.

Jellyfish are not actually fish. They are in the same phylum as coral and sea anemones.

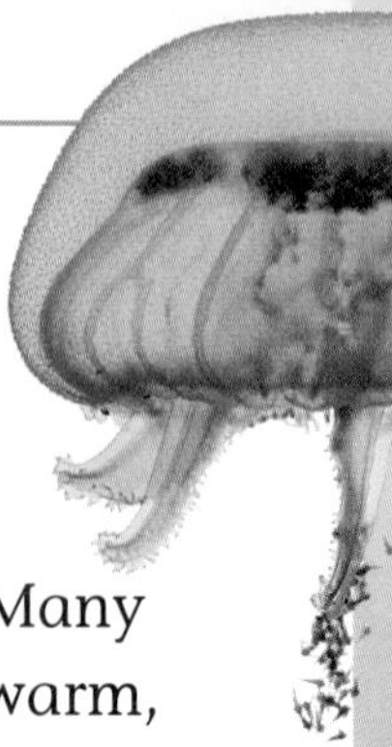

Coral Reefs

What ocean animals can you list? Many animals on your list probably live in warm, shallow waters around coral reefs. Because so many organisms live around them, coral reefs are like busy cities in the ocean. Around a reef, divers may see sharks, clams, crabs, clownfish, eels, and many other animals.

Corals are animals that have a special relationship with algae. Some algae carry on photosynthesis. They grow only in shallow, warm waters. If the water is too deep, sunlight will not reach them. These algae grow inside the coral. Others help the coral grow and build its skeleton. As corals grow and die, their hard skeletal parts pile up to make the reef. The nooks and crannies of the reef are homes for many kinds of plants and animals.

Coral reefs grow well in water that does not have many nutrients. Extra nutrients may actually harm a coral reef by helping the coral's enemies grow. Corals also need to be in water that is about 18°C or warmer. Reefs are found near the coasts of Florida, Australia, and many other places.

Coral reefs are important ecosystems. They often protect shore lines from ocean storms. The organisms found here have provided new kinds of medicines. Many kinds of food are found along reefs.

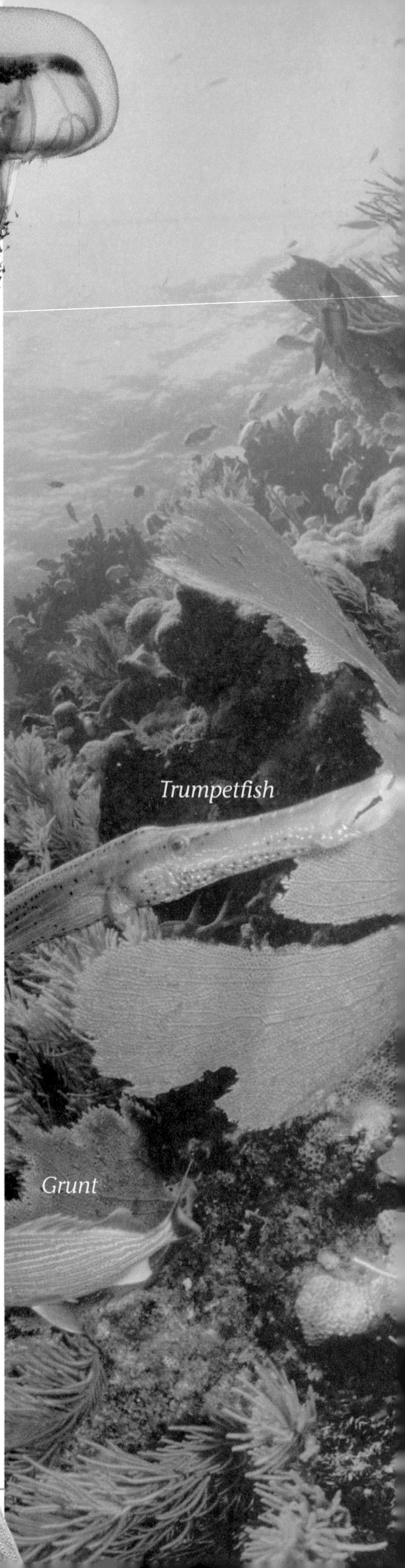
Trumpetfish
Grunt

Brain coral colonies can grow to be as large as 2 meters across.

Map Fact

The first deep-sea vent was discovered in 1977 near the Galapagos Islands. In these vents, water as hot as 400°C rushes out of the ocean floor.

This fish lives about 1,000 meters below the surface. Special organs scattered over its body make the fish glow in the dark.

The Deep Sea

In the deeper areas of the ocean, you find some very strange creatures. These creatures have to deal with cold, darkness, and very high water pressure.

Sunlight cannot reach these cold depths, so no plants can grow. Many animals eat dead plants and animals that sink from higher levels. In other places, called deep-sea vents, bacteria make food from chemicals in the water. These bacteria are then eaten by bigger animals. Clams, crabs, and tubeworms also live around the vents.

Far below the ocean waves, the water pressure is very great. Amazingly, the animals' bodies are adapted for living under this crushing pressure. When the animals are lifted to the surface where the pressure is less, the animals die.

√ Lesson Checkpoint

1. Why do coral live only in shallow water?
2. How does the type of water found in a water ecosystem affect the kind of organisms that live there?
3. **Art in Science** Research an estuary and another water ecosystem. Make a poster to show where the ecosystems are, the kind of water in them, and how the water flows.

Tubeworms don't have a mouth or stomach. Bacteria live inside the tubeworms and make food that they share.

Lesson 4

How do organisms interact?

Plants and animals interact with each other. Sometimes their interactions are helpful. Sometimes, they are not.

Competition Among Animals

Have you ever competed in a sport? The prize for winning a sports event may be a trophy or just the pride of winning. The cost of losing is simply disappointment. In the world of animals, stakes of competition are much greater.

In all environments, organisms may compete for the things they need. They may compete over space, water, light, food, or mates. They do not compete for a trophy. They often compete for their lives. An organism that cannot compete may die or may be forced to move away to get its needs met.

Animals of the same species sometimes compete with one another. At other times, different species compete for resources. For example, rabbits, mice, and other animals of a desert community compete with each other for food plants.

Animals such as cats, dogs, and bears may compete for territory. You may have heard cats screeching as they fight over territory in your neighborhood. Perhaps you have heard a dog's loud bark when it sees a person in its yard. This is the dog's way of warning, "Get out of my territory!"

Competition Among Plants

Have you heard of the plant that ate the South? This is what many people have jokingly said about kudzu, a vine that was brought to southern states in the mid-1880s. When it competes with other plants for sunlight, kudzu usually wins. The vine quickly grows and covers other plants, preventing them from getting sunlight. Since the covered plants cannot move away, they die.

Plants may also compete for water. Plants with larger root systems will absorb water more quickly than other plants. In what kind of biome do you think this competition is strongest?

Black bears will compete with each other for territory and mates.

These sheep are competing by hitting their horns together.

Plants may compete for sunlight. Kudzu, shown here, often covers other plants in this competition.

1. **Checkpoint** Describe why organisms compete and what the results of competition might be.
2. **Math in Science** How many years ago was kudzu brought to the southern states?

Symbiosis—Living Together

Animals are not always in competition with each other. Just as there are many kinds of relationships between people, there are many kinds of relationships between species. Symbiosis is a long-term relationship between different species. One of the species is always helped. The other might be helped, harmed, or not affected at all.

The buffalo and the cattle egret show one kind of symbiosis. As the buffalo grazes, it causes insects hiding in the grass to fly or hop away. The bird can easily get a meal by feeding on these moving insects. In this kind of symbiosis, the bird is helped and the buffalo is not really affected. Egrets may eat insects off the back of buffalo, but whether or not this helps the buffalo is not certain.

A second kind of symbiosis does help the buffalo. Microorganisms inside its digestive system help the buffalo digest the food it eats. In this kind of symbiosis, both species are helped. The tiny creatures have a meal brought to them, and the buffalo can digest grass and leaves.

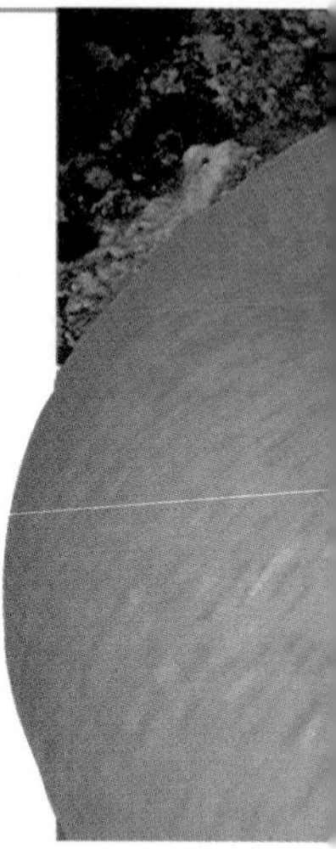

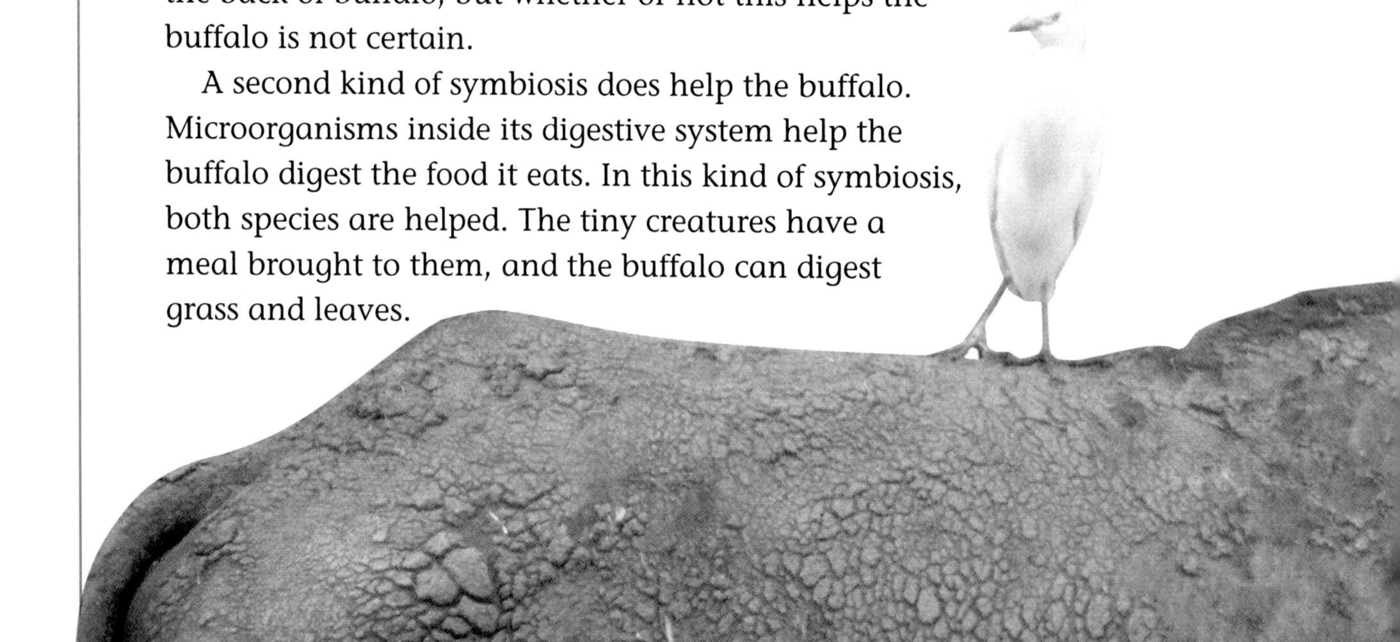

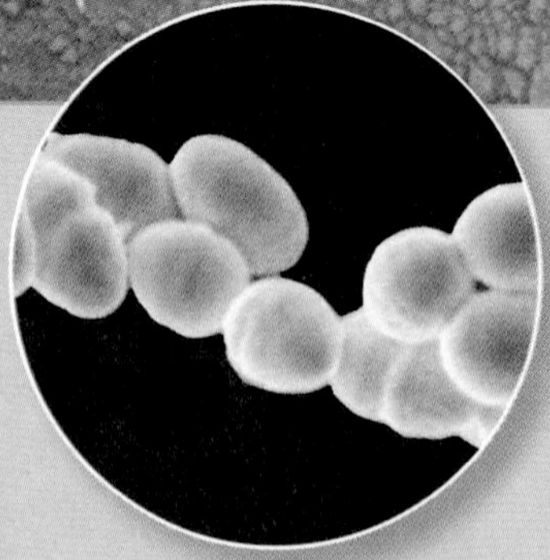

Bacteria and protists help buffalo, cows, sheep, elk, and other animals digest grass and other plants.

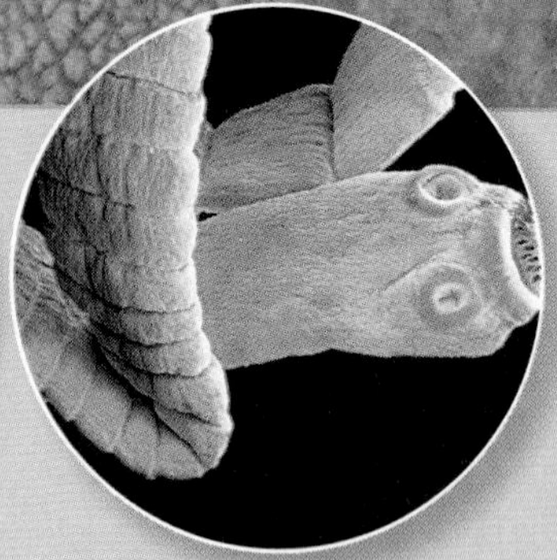

There are many kinds of tapeworms that live in the intestines of many kinds of animals.

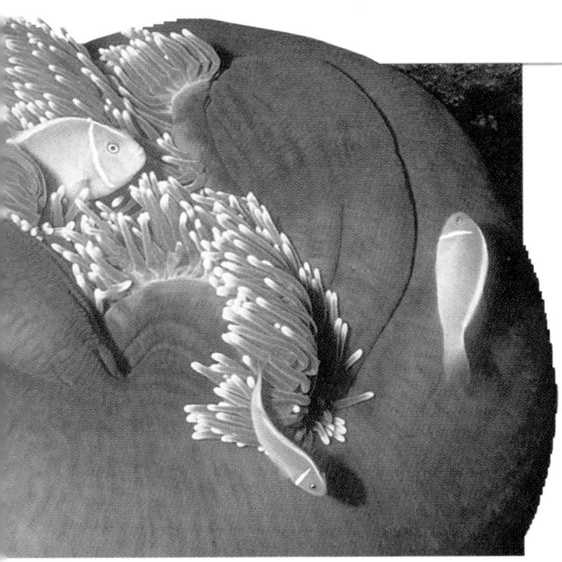

The relationship between the clownfish and sea anemone is an example of symbiosis. When the fish is among the anemone's tentacles, the anemone will sting any fish that attacks the clownfish. The anemone gets food from the clownfish by eathing leftovers attached to the clownfish's body.

Helpful or Harmful

In a third kind of symbiosis, organisms might cause the buffalo great harm. These organisms are parasites. A parasite is an organism that feeds off another organism, called a host. Some parasites are worms that live in the buffalo's intestines or bloodstream. These parasites eat the buffalo's food before the food gets to the buffalo's cells. They also might take oxygen from the buffalo's blood. Parasites can make the buffalo weak and sick.

In another kind of symbiosis, one organism is not just helped by a partner, but rather it needs a partner in order to survive. Lichen is one example. It is made up of a fungus and a plant-like bacteria or algae. The bacteria or algae make food from sunlight. The fungus survives by getting some of this food. The fungus gives the bacteria or algae a safe home.

✓ Lesson Checkpoint

1. Describe the symbiosis between a parasite and its host.
2. Give an example of a relationship where both organisms are helped.
3. **Predict** Suppose a veterinarian gave a buffalo some medicine that killed all organisms inside the buffalo. Predict what effects this would have on the buffalo.

Lesson 5

How does energy move in ecosystems?

Energy can pass through an ecosystem when food is eaten, but some energy is always changed to heat and not passed on.

Energy from Food

Every organism needs energy in order to live. Energy moves through an ecosystem through food chains, energy chains, or food webs.

Plants, protists, and other microorganisms are producers. Producers make their own food for energy. They get energy to make food from the energy of sunlight or chemicals in nature. Many other organisms use food that producers make.

Consumers cannot make their own food. They usually eat other organisms to get energy to live and grow. All animals are consumers. There are several kinds of consumers. Herbivores eat only plants. Carnivores, also called predators, eat only other animals, which are their prey. Omnivores eat both plants and animals. Decomposers eat waste or dead organisms.

Northern Spotted Owl

When an animal eats, it takes in matter as well as the energy stored in food. Arrows in the food chain below show how energy can flow through an ecosystem from a producer to an herbivore, a carnivore, and finally to a decomposer. You can see that the energy the spotted owl gets from eating the hare came from plants.

Sun → plants → snowshoe hare → spotted owl → bacteria

Insects

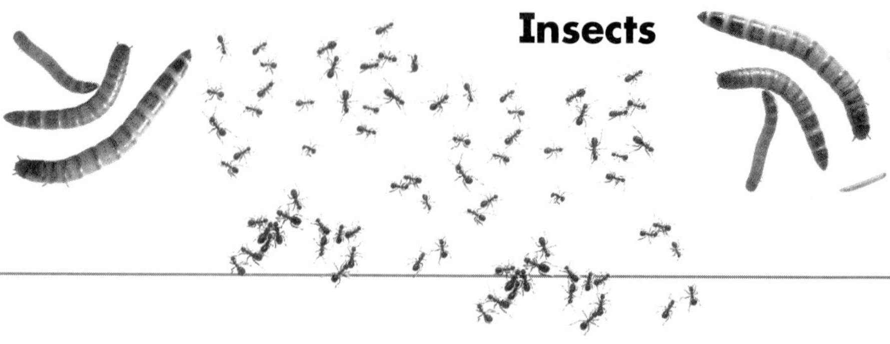

Food Chains and Webs

On land, most animal food can be traced back in some way to plants. In the ocean, food chains often start with plant-like microorganisms called plankton. Food chains at deep-sea vents start with bacteria.

Food chains can be very short, involving only a plant and a decomposer. Chains can also be longer, involving more than one carnivore. A food chain is not a complete way of describing energy flow in an ecosystem. This is because consumers usually eat many kinds of other organisms. To see an ecosystem more fully, you need to look at a food web like the one below. A food web combines many food chains into one picture.

1. **Checkpoint** What is the niche, or role, of a producer?
2. **Art in Science** Draw a diagram showing the sequence of organisms feeding in a food web. Your diagram may have organisms of your choosing. Describe how your diagram shows the flow of matter and energy.

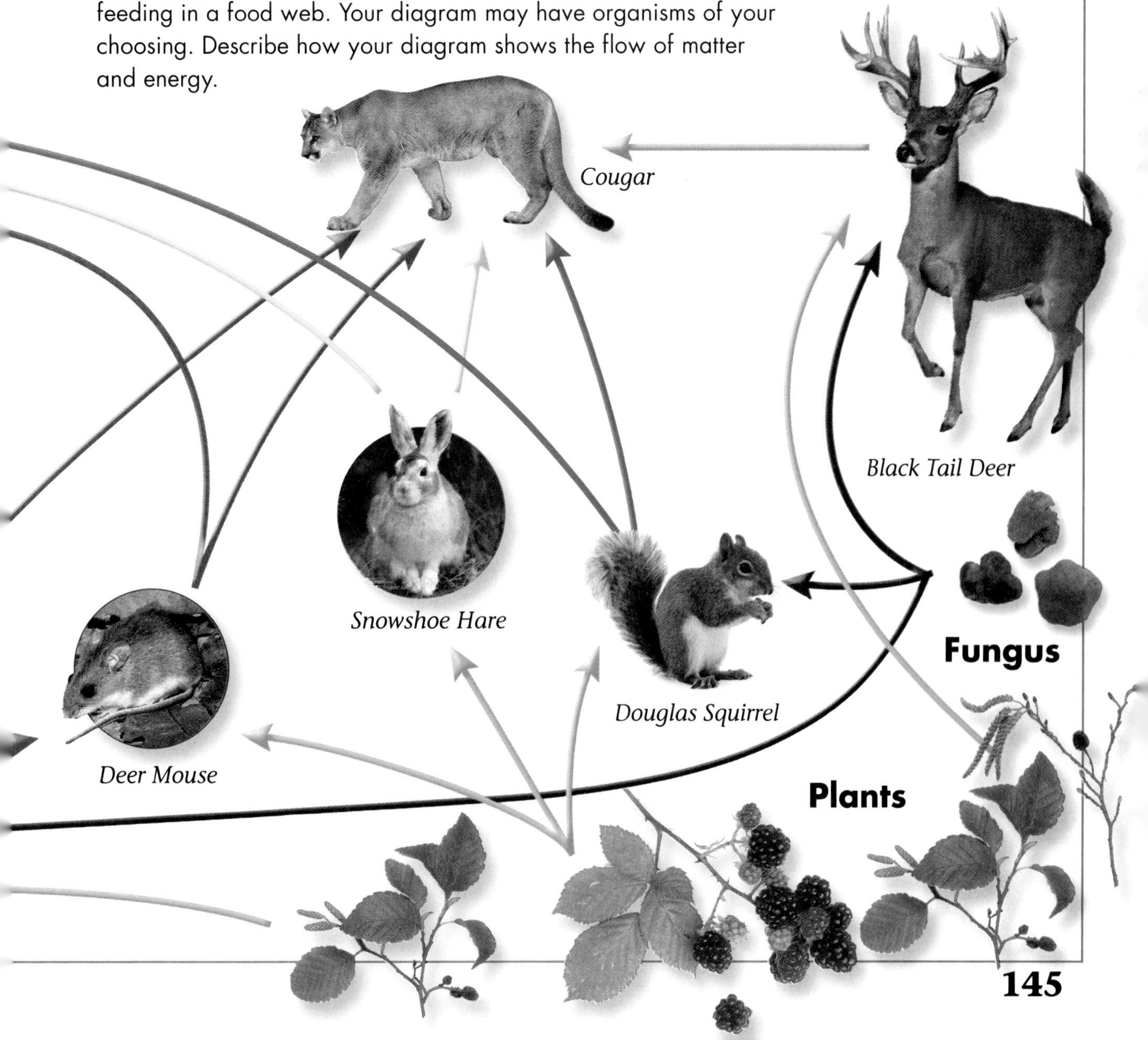

Cougar
Black Tail Deer
Snowshoe Hare
Douglas Squirrel
Deer Mouse
Fungus
Plants

Energy Pyramids

In an ecosystem, energy flows from the Sun to producers to herbivores and carnivores. However, most of the energy within every organism does not reach the next organism in the food chain.

An **energy pyramid** is a diagram that shows the amounts of energy that flow through each level of a food chain. The base of the energy pyramid is widest. This shows the energy in the producers. Producers have the greatest amount of energy in an ecosystem. Notice that the pyramid becomes narrower at the upper levels. This shows that less energy flows upward from the lower levels to the higher ones. Decomposers are not shown in energy pyramids.

Some energy cannot flow upward in the pyramid because most of the energy has been changed. The energy does not disappear. Organisms use most of the energy to warm their bodies and do activities. Their bodies store only a small amount of energy. Only stored energy can pass along the food chain. For example, a snowshoe hare gets energy by eating plants. The hare uses its food's energy to run, breathe, and do other life activities. These activities turn most energy from the rabbit's food into body heat. By the time an owl eats the hare, only a part of the plants' energy can pass along in the food chain.

√ Lesson Checkpoint

1. Explain how an energy pyramid shows the flow of energy in a food chain or food web.
2. Explain why an animal's food and energy can be traced back to plants and the Sun.
3. **Writing in Science** **Expository** In your **science journal,** write directions to younger students explaining how to draw food chains and food webs. In your directions, use and define the words *producer, consumer, herbivore, carnivore, omnivore,* and *decomposer*.

Owls get energy from eating animals. Only a small fraction of the energy in the owls' food is stored in their bodies.
Heat
Snowshoe hares get energy from plants. Only a small amount of this energy is stored in their bodies.
Heat
Plants get energy from sunlight. They store some of this energy.
Heat

Lesson 6

What cycles occur in ecosystems?

In an ecosystem, a substance may be passed from one organism to another. These substances go through an ecosystem again and again.

Recycling Matter

Every day in every ecosystem, animals produce waste products. Eventually plants, animals, and all other organisms will die. There must be a way to "clean up" the waste and dead matter.

With its yellow coloring and long body, it is not hard to see why this is called the banana slug. As it eats material on the forest floor, this decomposer can grow to be 25 centimeters long.

A fungus breaks down a log by releasing special chemicals. Materials from the log are then absorbed by the fungus and used as food.

Decomposers are organisms that eat wastes and dead matter. By doing this, they break material into smaller pieces and put it back into the soil. Most decomposers are microorganisms like bacteria and fungi. Earthworms, flies, and slugs are also decomposers. Whenever you see something decaying or rotting, decomposers have been at work.

Decomposers have the important niche, or role, of recycling wastes and dead material. Decomposers change the wastes and dead material into minerals and nutrients that plants can use. These plants will then be food for other organisms. In this way, minerals and nutrients become part of a cycle. A **cycle** is a repeating process or a repeating flow of material through a system. There is a constant cycle of minerals and some nutrients moving from living things to the soil and back into living things.

Decomposers are not the only things that break down dead matter. Fire also does this. When plants burn, their ashes become part of the soil.

1. ✓ **Checkpoint** What is the niche of slime molds and other decomposers?
2. **Math in Science** A slug started moving across a log at 10:52 A.M. and got to the other end at 11:09 A.M. How many minutes did the slug take to cross the log?

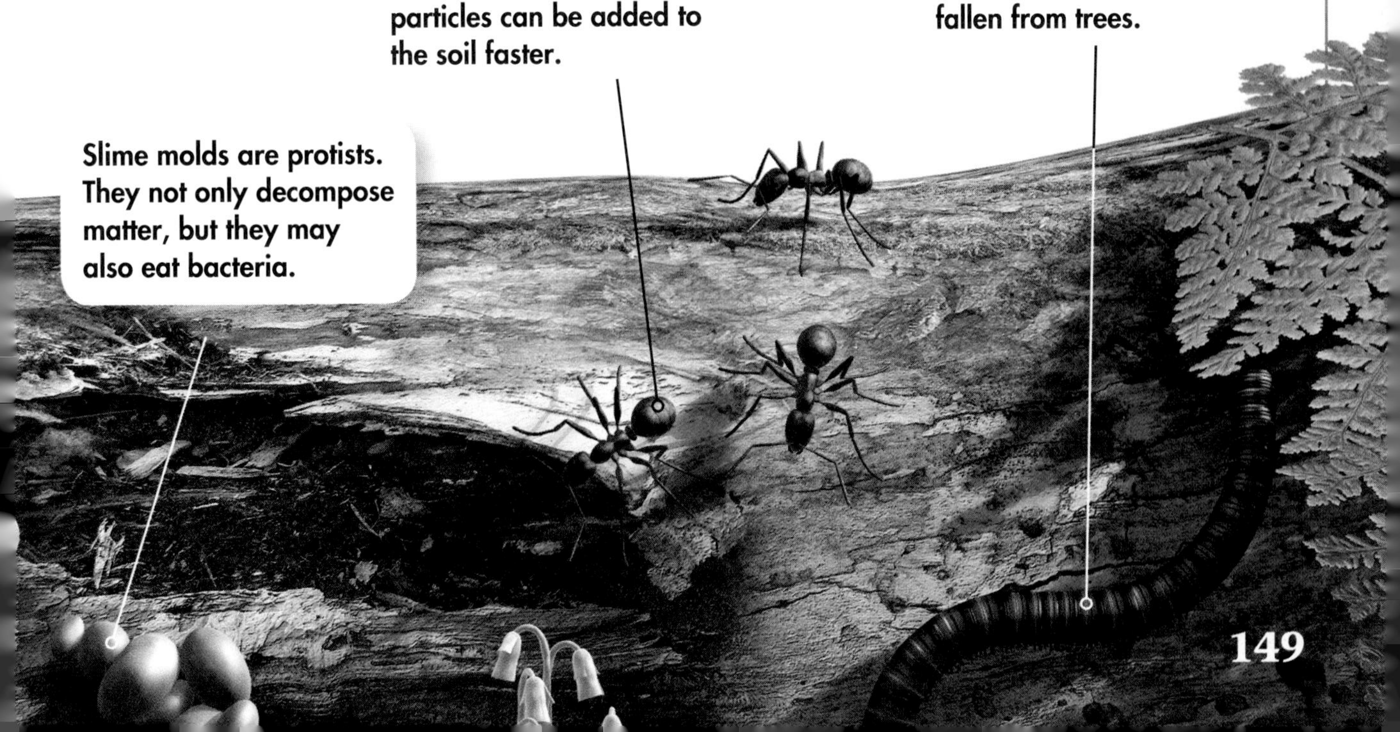

Carpenter ants do not eat wood, but they do chew through it to make their homes. The resulting wood particles can be added to the soil faster.

The almond-scented millipede eats pine needles and other leaves that have fallen from trees.

Slime molds are protists. They not only decompose matter, but they may also eat bacteria.

Nitrogen Cycle

Cells in plants and animals need nitrogen to do their work. Nitrogen cycles through ecosystems. It moves through the food chain and other processes.

Nitrogen is all around us. Almost $\frac{8}{10}$ of Earth's atmosphere is nitrogen gas. Most organisms cannot use nitrogen gas from the air. They must use nitrogen compounds, which are chemicals that contain nitrogen. Nitrogen compounds form in many ways.

A bromeliad is a plant that contains certain bacteria. These bacteria can make nitrogen compounds from nitrogen in the air.

Only a part of the nitrogen cycle is shown here.

How Nitrogen Compounds Form

Nitrogen compounds can form in the atmosphere. Lightning can cause nitrogen to combine with other gases in air and make nitrogen compounds. Rain carries these compounds to Earth's soil and water.

Nitrogen in Ecosystems

Some kinds of bacteria make nitrogen compounds and put them into the soil. Plant roots absorb the compounds along with the water in the soil.

Some plants in tropical rainforests contain bacteria that make nitrogen compounds. These plants grow in the upper branches of the trees in the forest. Bacteria living in special roots are able to take in nitrogen directly from the air.

Herbivores get the nitrogen they need when they eat plants. Carnivores get nitrogen when they eat the herbivores. Nitrogen returns to the soil or air when animals and plants die. It also returns in animals' waste products. Decomposers break down the remains of dead organisms and waste products. They change the animals' nitrogen compounds into kinds that plants can use. The compounds return to the soil or air and the cycle repeats.

People add nitrogen compounds to the soil. Many farmers use fertilizers that contain nitrogen. Fertilizers are materials that make soil better for growing crops. Nitrogen fertilizers are important to society. They help farmers grow more food in their fields.

The Nitrogen Cycle

Herbivores get nitrogen compounds when they eat plants.
Carnivores get nitrogen compounds when they eat herbivores.
Lightning produces nitrogen compounds from gases in the air.
Microorganisms make nitrogen compounds and put them in soil.
Plants absorb nitrogen compounds from the soil.
Nitrogen returns to the soil or air when organisms or wastes decompose. Decomposers may change these compounds into materials that plants can use.

1. **√Checkpoint** Describe how matter cycles through an ecosystem.
2. **Social Studies in Science** Use library, Internet, or other resources to learn how society and the environment have been changed by the use of fertilizers containing nitrogen. Write what you learn in your **science journal.**

Carbon Dioxide and Oxygen

Oxygen is the second most abundant gas in the atmosphere. It makes up about $\frac{2}{10}$ of the air. There is much less carbon dioxide. It makes up less than $\frac{1}{100}$ of the air. Even so, there is enough carbon dioxide to meet the needs of all the world's plants.

Carbon dioxide and oxygen gases are always being made and used in the world's ecosystems. You have learned that plants take in carbon dioxide and give off oxygen, and animals take in oxygen and give off carbon dioxide. But the use of these gases is not as simple as that. As this diagram shows, the give-and-take of oxygen and carbon dioxide has many paths through an ecosystem.

In the process of photosynthesis, plants use carbon dioxide with water and release oxygen.
Trucks, cars, power plants, and many other machines run by burning fuel. During burning, oxygen is used and carbon dioxide is released.

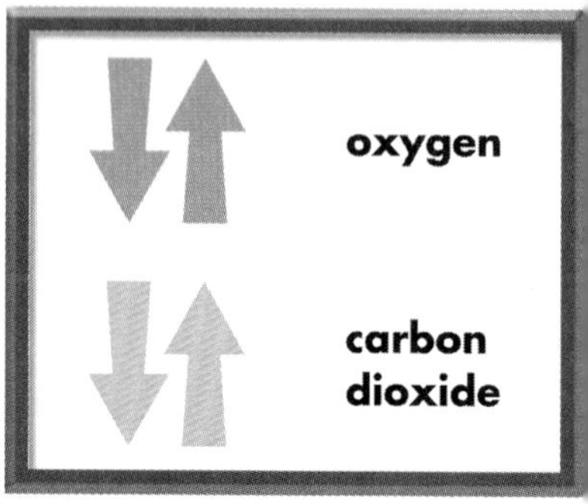

oxygen
carbon dioxide

Using and Releasing Gases

Oxygen can enter the air during photosynthesis. Many kinds of organisms besides plants make oxygen by photosynthesis. Some microscopic organisms in the ocean, called plankton, carry out photosynthesis. Some kinds of bacteria and protists also can make oxygen by photosynthesis.

Carbon dioxide also enters the atmosphere in many ways. Two major ways are through cellular respiration and combustion.

Remember that cellular respiration is a process that cells use to get energy. In respiration, cells combine oxygen with food. The results of respiration are carbon dioxide and water. Plants and animals, both on land and in water, live by respiration.

Combustion is the burning of a material. Carbon dioxide forms as a result of combustion. Combustion occurs naturally, such as in forest fires. It also occurs in machines, such as cars, power plants, and home furnaces.

When trees and other plants burn, fire takes oxygen from the air and gives off carbon dioxide.
In all the cells of plants and animals, the process of cellular respiration uses oxygen with sugar and releases carbon dioxide.
Volcanoes spew out more than just lava and ash. They also release huge amounts of carbon dioxide.
Oxygen and carbon dioxide are dissolved in the water of rain, oceans, lakes, and rivers. Organisms in the water can use these gases in respiration and photosynthesis.
Carbon dioxide is released when materials are decomposed.
Some oxygen gets removed from the air when it combines with materials. For example, oxygen combines with iron to make rust.
Plants are a major source of the oxygen in the atmosphere. Much of the oxygen in the atmosphere, though, does not come from plants. It comes from plankton in the oceans.

√ Lesson Checkpoint

1. Describe three ways that oxygen gas is removed from the atmosphere and used.
2. How is lightning helpful to organisms?
3. **Math in Science** The amount of nitrogen in the air is about how many times the amount of oxygen? Make an estimate.

Lab zone

Guided Inquiry

Investigate How can you show that plants use carbon dioxide?

Plants use carbon dioxide and give off oxygen. People use oxygen and give off carbon dioxide. In this investigation, you will observe this process by using a chemical called BTB. BTB turns greenish yellow when there is a high level of carbon dioxide. BTB turns blue when there is a low level of carbon dioxide.

Materials

safety goggles

cup and drinking straw

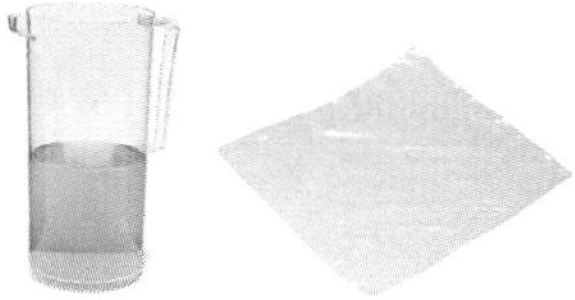

water with BTB and plastic wrap

elodea

What to Do

1 Fill a cup $\frac{1}{3}$ full of water with BTB. Cover with plastic wrap.

Be careful!

Wear safety goggles. Do not drink the water with BTB.

$\frac{1}{3}$ full

2 **Investigate** to show that plants use carbon dioxide. Push the straw through the plastic wrap. Gently breathe *out* through the straw into the water. Stop as soon as the color starts to change.

Use the straw to breathe out only! Do not breathe in.

Process Skills

When you conduct a scientific **investigation**, you carry out a careful procedure to answer a question.

3 Record how the color changes.

4 Put the elodea into the water. Put the cup in a bright place. **Observe** every 10 minutes. Record how the color changes.

	Color of Water with BTB
Before breathing out into the water	
After breathing out into the water	
After adding elodea to the water	

BTB indicates how much carbon dioxide is in the water.

greenish yellow = high level of carbon dioxide

blue = low level of carbon dioxide

Explain Your Results

1. What made the color of the water with BTB change when you breathed into it?
2. In your **investigation,** what made the color change after you added the elodea?

Go Further

What would happen if the elodea and water with BTB were put in a dark place? Write a procedure others could follow to answer this question.

Math in Science

Population Cycles

How do the populations of predators and their prey affect each other? Answering this question is very difficult. There are many things that can affect the size of a population.

Scientists use special computer programs called models to predict population changes. The models use data for just one population each of predators and prey living in a perfect habitat. The graph below shows one model's prediction of the cycle, or repeating pattern, of growth and decline during one month. The populations go up and down within a certain range.

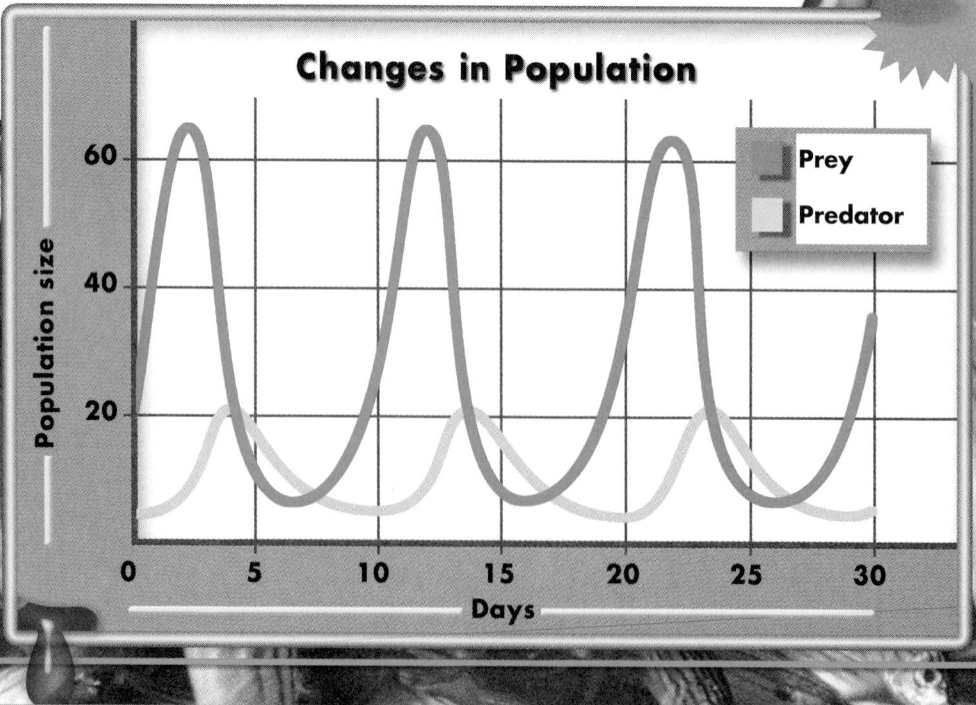

Changes in Population
Prey
Predator
60
40
20
Population size
0
5
10
15
20
25
30
Days

Use the graph of the population cycles to answer these questions.

1. When is the population of prey the greatest?
A. days 1, 13, and 25
B. days 7, 14, and 21
C. days 2, 12, and 22
D. days 2, 5, and 8

2. Which is a reasonable estimate for the difference between the greatest and the least number of predators?
F. 5 G. 10 H. 16 I. 22

3. Which compares the greatest population of prey to the greatest population of predators?
A. There are more than 3 times as many prey as predators.
B. There are about twice as many prey as predators.
C. There are about 10 more prey than predators.
D. The populations are the same.

4. What happens after the predator's population becomes greater than the prey's?
F. This never happens.
G. The prey's population quickly decreases to zero.
H. Both populations decrease.
I. The prey's population immediately increases.

Lab zone Take-Home Activity

Keep a record of the amount of some type of food that is used each day in your home. Also, record the number of people who use this food each day. After one week of recording, graph your data.

Chapter 5 Review and Test Prep

Use Vocabulary

community (p. 127)	**energy pyramid** (p. 146)
cycle (p. 149)	**habitat** (p. 129)
ecosystem (p. 127)	**niche** (p. 129)
	population (p. 127)

Use the term from the list above that best completes each sentence.

1. A(n) _____ is one way of showing the amount of energy available at each stage of a food chain.

2. The place in an ecosystem where an organism normally lives is its _____.

3. A(n) _____ is the combination of living and non-living things and their interactions.

4. All of the populations of organisms in a(n) _____ belong to different species but live the same area.

5. The role each organism has in an ecosystem is its _____.

6. A group of organisms of the same species living in one area is a(n) _____.

7. Materials often repeat a pattern, or _____, as they move through different parts of an ecosystem.

Explain Concepts

8. Explain how energy and materials move through an ecosystem.

9. Explain ways that organisms interact in helpful and harmful ways.

10. Explain the flow of energy in an energy pyramid like the one below. Then tell how an energy pyramid and a food chain are the same and how they are different.

11. Explain how different structures or behaviors help organisms survive in their habitats.

12. Explain what a biome is. Describe four examples of biomes.

Process Skills

13. Estimate how many ants are on an entire sidewalk. Some students counted the number of ants on each of four sections of sidewalk. Their data is given in the table below. The sidewalk has a total of 20 sections. Explain how you estimated.

Section	Ants Counted
Section 1	6
Section 2	11
Section 3	10
Section 4	9

Predict

14. Predict A desert community has foxes, rabbits, and grasses. Predict what would happen to the population of grasses in this desert if the population of foxes increased.

Test Prep

Choose the letter that best completes the statement or answers the question.

15. Which of the following consists of parts working together?
- Ⓐ niche
- Ⓑ system
- Ⓒ population
- Ⓓ habitat

16. Which biome can be best described as an evergreen forest in a cold, dry location?
- Ⓕ taiga
- Ⓖ temperate rainforest
- Ⓗ tundra
- Ⓘ deciduous forest

17. Organisms can only live where
- Ⓐ there is sunlight.
- Ⓑ there is dry land.
- Ⓒ they can move around.
- Ⓓ their needs can be met.

18. What kind of organism helps clean a habitat of waste and dead remains?
- Ⓕ decomposer
- Ⓖ carnivore
- Ⓗ herbivore
- Ⓘ omnivore

19. Explain why the answer you select for Question 18 is best. For each of the answers you do not select, give a reason why it is not the best answer.

20. Writing in Science **Descriptive** Describe an ecosystem. List the living and nonliving parts and processes of the system. Discuss the niches of the organisms you list.

Greenhouse Manager

As a greenhouse manager, your job would be to create a good ecosystem for the plants inside a greenhouse. The manager of a greenhouse makes sure that the temperature is just right for the plants and that the plants have the right amounts of soil, food, water, and, of course, sunshine.

Because greenhouses sell many different types of plants, the greenhouse manager must create a good ecosystem for each one. This means adjusting the moisture levels and amounts of sunlight or shade to those best suited for each type of plant.

Greenhouses are small businesses. The greenhouse manager may hire, train, and supervise workers to help.

If you like working with plants and people, a career as a greenhouse manager can begin by completing a two-year college program in horticulture.

Lab zone Take-Home Activity

Choose a kind of seed to grow in your home. Read about the seed you choose so that you can provide a good ecosystem for the plant. When the plant has grown, show it to your class.